Guide for Implementing or Enhancing an Endangered Missing Advisory

March 2011
NCJ 232001

America's Missing:
Broadcast Emergency Response

This document was prepared under cooperative agreement number 2008–MC–CX–K028 from the Office of Juvenile Justice and Delinquency Prevention (OJJDP), U.S. Department of Justice. Points of view or opinions expressed in this document are those of the authors and do not necessarily represent the official position or policies of OJJDP or the U.S. Department of Justice.

U.S. Department of Justice

Office of Justice Programs

Office of the Assistant Attorney General

Washington, D.C. 20531

Message From Assistant Attorney General Laurie O. Robinson

As National AMBER Alert Coordinator, I have been privileged to work closely with our federal, tribal, state, local, and private-sector partners, who share the Department of Justice's goal of returning every missing child to the safety of his or her home. I am encouraged by the significant progress attained through our collaborative efforts.

At the same time, I remain concerned that the cases of missing children that do not meet the high threshold for the issuance of an AMBER Alert do not always receive the coordinated search efforts they deserve. The same concern applies to missing persons older than 18, who fall outside AMBER Alert's purview.

The Endangered Missing Advisory (EMA) was crafted in 2005 to fill this gap. At the time, only five states had a plan to address it. Today, 34 states have enacted EMA plans.

As AMBER Alerts are widely known, they have contributed greatly to the recovery of hundreds of missing children. However, there is little public awareness of the role played by EMAs and inadequate professional recognition of best practices regarding their implementation.

The information provided in these pages promotes these ends, and I commend it for your consideration.

Laurie O. Robinson
Assistant Attorney General

Foreword

The unauthorized absence of a child from the home is a family crisis that requires immediate and collaborative attention. Over the past two decades the AMBER Alert Program has grown into a nationally coordinated effort under the Office of Justice Programs, which has significantly improved the strategies and the methods for recovering endangered and abducted children. More than 500 children have been returned home as a result of AMBER Alert plans, which have been established in every state.

Despite such progress, however, gaps remain in the recovery of missing children whose cases do not meet the strict criteria for AMBER Alert and of missing adults, whose cases are not covered by AMBER Alert. To assist communities in closing these gaps, the Office of Juvenile Justice and Delinquency Prevention has initiated a project to help states, communities, and law enforcement agencies develop a strategy in which the Endangered Missing Advisory (EMA) plays a crucial role.

This guide provides AMBER Alert coordinators, law enforcement, and public safety professionals with an effective and efficient way to implement an EMA plan. It offers recommendations to assist law enforcement in developing strategies to recover missing children and adults and includes relevant findings to inform policymakers' efforts to address the problem.

It is my hope and conviction that adoption of the recommendations set forth in these pages will enable communities to implement a comprehensive and practical approach to recovering missing children and adults.

Jeff Slowikowski
Acting Administrator
Office of Juvenile Justice and Delinquency Prevention

This document was prepared under cooperative agreement number 2008–MC–CX–K028 from the Office of Juvenile Justice and Delinquency Prevention (OJJDP), U.S. Department of Justice. Points of view or opinions expressed in this document are those of the authors and do not necessarily represent the official position or policies of OJJDP or the U.S. Department of Justice.

Guide for Implementing or Enhancing an Endangered Missing Advisory

March 2011
NCJ 232001

America's Missing:
Broadcast Emergency Response

Contents

Implementing or Enhancing an Endangered Missing Advisory

Introduction

On February 2, 2004, 11-year-old Carlie Brucia called her parents from a friend's house to tell them she was on her way home. When she did not show up, Carlie's parents called the police and reported their daughter missing. Because the police did not have evidence that Carlie was abducted, they did not issue an AMBER Alert. The police suspected that Carlie may have run away. The following day, the owner of a carwash near Carlie's home found a disturbing scene on the facility's surveillance video. It showed a husky man snatching Carlie's arm and whisking her away. Once the authorities viewed the video, an AMBER Alert was issued immediately. Unfortunately, critical time had been lost. Joseph Smith, a man with a long criminal history, raped Carlie and strangled her to death. He left her body near a church located a mile from the carwash. He was caught, convicted, and sentenced to death.

The Carlie Brucia case and many others like it raised the question: what can be done in a situation that does not meet the strict criteria of the AMBER Alert Program? This guide is offered as a resource to law enforcement and child protection professionals to answer this question.

The AMBER Alert Program began in 1997. During the first 6 years of the program, the alert saved a total of 31 children. In 2003, President George W. Bush signed the Prosecutorial Remedies and Other Tools to End the Exploitation of Children Today (PROTECT) Act. This comprehensive child protection legislation called for the creation of a national, seamless network of AMBER coordinators. Through federal funding, at least 120 local, regional, tribal, and state AMBER Alert plans are in operation today, including statewide plans in every state.

The U.S. Department of Justice (DOJ), Office of Justice Programs, developed general recommended criteria for law enforcement agencies to use and/or modify for their specific needs to help first responders and officers determine whether an AMBER Alert should be issued when a child is reported missing. The efficiency of the program and the number of children rescued by alerts increased dramatically after these criteria were standardized and the program was adopted nationwide.

The AMBER Alert system has succeeded beyond all expectations. From 2003 to August 2010, AMBER Alerts helped directly in the safe recovery of 518 children in the United States.[1] However, AMBER Alerts are not issued for individuals who do not meet the criteria. In these cases, states and local communities that want to take a proactive role in helping rescue missing and endangered persons might consider developing or enhancing an Endangered Missing Advisory (EMA).

EMAs are now being adopted across the country in a manner that is similar to that of the AMBER Alert. A 2005 survey found that five states had formal response plans for cases that did not meet the AMBER Alert criteria. In 2006, DOJ initiated the Endangered Missing Persons Project, which encouraged the development of a nationwide plan. A 2009 survey found that 34 states had formal EMA plans—16 states without age restrictions and 18 states with age restrictions. Most plans with age restrictions involve senior citizens.

States with an EMA plan offered numerous examples of children and adults who were recovered after an advisory was issued (exact numbers are not available because advisories are not subject to the same reporting requirements as AMBER Alerts). More detailed information will become

---

[1] As recorded by the National Center for Missing & Exploited Children.

available as EMA plans become standardized (Murphy, 2009).

How To Use This Document

The EMA, which is similar to the AMBER Alert, brings together law enforcement agencies, broadcasters, transportation agencies, and others in a voluntary partnership to enlist the aid of the public in finding a missing person. The EMA can be issued to help find a missing person who may be in danger but does not fit the AMBER Alert criteria.

This guide offers issues for consideration, potential problems, and recommended partnerships to establish a task force and set up an EMA plan. The first section of the guide focuses on developing an EMA plan, and the second section discusses the steps involved in activating an EMA. The final section addresses the critical issues of building and sustaining support for the EMA plan. The guide also features examples of EMA plans, press releases, and real-life examples of how the EMA was used to help save missing people.

What Is the Endangered Missing Advisory?

The EMA is a tool that gives law enforcement and other key partners a formal action plan to safely recover missing children who do not fit the AMBER Alert criteria. It also provides a way to help recover missing adults in cases where no systematic recovery plan exists. Law enforcement can choose between AMBER and EMA based on the individual case and the appropriate criteria.

The EMA is designed to provide a rapid response to safely recover missing persons who may be in danger. Issuance of an EMA can help raise awareness of the dangers that missing persons face and reduce the pressure on police to issue an AMBER Alert in cases that do not fit the criteria. More important, the EMA provides a strategy for law enforcement to notify the public and save lives.

Many missing children do not fit the criteria for an AMBER Alert but may, nonetheless, be endangered. The federal government's most comprehensive report found that 1,682,900 youth either ran away from home or were thrown away by their caretaker during a single year. An estimated 1,190,900 youth (71 percent) could have been endangered because of substance abuse, sexual or physical abuse, the presence of criminal activity, or because the child was age 13 or younger (Office of Juvenile Justice and Delinquency Prevention, 2002).

Another study found that 68.7 percent of all child abduction homicides began as a missing child or runaway report (McKenna, 2006). This study found that one out of five child abduction homicide victims are already dead before police are even notified.

A strategy such as the EMA, which can be issued more quickly than an AMBER Alert, can be used to notify the public in a timely manner while investigators determine whether a case meets the AMBER Alert criteria. A 2007 report shows that of 227 AMBER Alerts, 4 (2 percent) were issued within the first hour of the child being reported abducted or missing, 36 (16 percent) were issued during the first 3 hours, and 44 (19 percent) were issued within the first 24 hours (National Center for Missing & Exploited Children, 2007). Meanwhile, nearly half (44 percent) of children in child abduction homicides are dead in less than an hour after abduction. In child abduction cases where homicide is the outcome, three out of four children are murdered within the first 3 hours (Washington State Office of the Attorney General, 1997). Time is the enemy in child abduction cases, and the first few hours are critical in the investigation. However, most child abductions do not end in homicide, and every effort should be made to find the child no matter how long he or she has been missing.

Because adults do not fit the AMBER Alert criteria but may be missing and endangered, they may benefit from a different type of alert system. According to the Alzheimer's Association, an estimated 5.2 million people have Alzheimer's disease. The association reports that 6 out of 10 people with Alzheimer's disease will wander from their homes or care facilities and as many as half of them will suffer serious injury or death if they are not found within 24 hours (Alzheimer's Association Statement on Silver Alert, 2008).

When an EMA is initiated, the following should take place:

+ Notification of local law enforcement and the media.

+ Distribution of fliers with photographs and information.

+ Notification of local residents by automated phone calls.

+ Activation of a Child Abduction Response Team (CART), if appropriate.

+ Notification of the National Crime Information Center (NCIC) if the person is younger than age 21.

+ Preparation of search and rescue teams for response.

Developing an EMA Plan

To develop an EMA plan, a jurisdiction must do the following:

+ Establish a task force.

+ Select a title for the plan.

+ Select the type of plan.

+ Establish criteria for the EMA.

+ Determine responsibilities for law enforcement agencies.

+ Coordinate with the Child Abduction Response Team.

+ Develop a major case-response plan.

+ Coordinate activation of the plan.

+ Establish an EMA protocol for news agencies.

+ Decide on a review board.

+ Develop and implement training for law enforcement and the media.

+ Test the EMA plan.

+ Coordinate press announcements.

+ Develop contact lists.

Each of these tasks is discussed below.

Establish a Task Force

Since every state has an AMBER Alert plan, the components of an EMA task force may already be in place. The task force should include key AMBER Alert stakeholders, such as representatives from federal, state, and local law enforcement agencies; emergency communication committee members; broadcasters and representatives from media outlets; and transportation and emergency management personnel. Law enforcement representatives should be informed that it does not cost anything to issue an EMA and media representatives should be assured that an EMA is voluntary and provided as a public service.

It is critical to cultivate good relationships with the media because a plan will not work without their cooperation. Broadcast general managers, operations managers, program directors, and news directors are important contacts because they are the decisionmakers for their organizations. The president of the broadcasters association in a state or the Radio Television Digital News Association can act as a liaison for broadcasters. Newspaper editors and media webmasters are also important because many people use the Internet to obtain information. Members of the EMA task force should also determine if there are any CARTs in the area and, if so, work closely with them.

In addition, state legislators, congressional representatives, and other community leaders can provide valuable support when an EMA is implemented. They can help create public awareness about the issue and how the EMA works. Their involvement may also help prevent any legislation or ordinances that may interfere or cause confusion when implementing the plan.

Ultimately, individuals involved in implementing an EMA should remember that it is a tool that can assist law enforcement with a critical missing person investigation. Law enforcement authorities will ultimately decide when and how to best use this tool.

The task force is responsible for the following:

+ Developing criteria and procedures for the EMA.

+ Strategically launching the EMA.

+ Providing training and technical assistance for law enforcement, the media, and the community on how to use the EMA appropriately.

+ Overseeing the EMA's operation and effectiveness.

+ Ensuring that EMAs are distributed in a timely fashion.

+ Developing ways to test and ensure that notifications are effective.

+ Creating materials that incorporate the EMA into AMBER Alert training.

+ Cultivating good public relations for the EMA.

+ Meeting regularly to review and evaluate procedures.

+ Chronicling the successes and shortcomings of the plan.

Select a Title for the Plan

Deciding on a title for an EMA plan can be a difficult task. The goal is to choose a title that does not cause confusion about the notification of an AMBER Alert. "AMBER Alert" has become a name associated with abducted children, and the title of the EMA plan should not dilute the power or the effectiveness of the AMBER Alert notification.

Like an AMBER Alert, the title should convey that a person is missing, in danger, and in need of a coordinated and public effort to ensure their safe recovery. The ultimate goal is for all states to eventually adopt a single title that will be recognized immediately when a person is missing and in danger.

Select the Type of Plan

The task force members should decide whether a plan will be most effective if it is local, regional, or statewide. The type of plan selected should be based on the current AMBER Alert plan; the presence of leadership to implement and coordinate the plan or event; the area's geography, population, and specific community needs; and the broadcast reach of television and radio stations. Certain critical missing cases require statewide coverage while others may require more localized coverage.

Establish Criteria for the EMA

The task force members should decide on the criteria for determining when to implement the EMA. The following criteria have been adopted by many states:

+ Do the circumstances fail to meet the criteria for an AMBER Alert? (If they do meet the criteria for an AMBER Alert, immediately follow the protocol to issue an AMBER Alert.)

+ Is the person missing under unexplained or suspicious circumstances?

+ Is the person believed to be in danger because of age, health, mental or physical disability, and environment or weather conditions; is he or she in the company of a potentially dangerous person; or is there any other factor that may put the person in peril?

+ Is there information that could assist the public in the safe recovery of the missing person?

The task force may choose to expand or limit the criteria, depending on the types of circumstances it wants to include for activation and how often notifications are desired.

Determine Responsibilities for Law Enforcement Agencies

Law enforcement agencies usually have protocols for investigating cases involving missing persons and abductions. The EMA can easily become a key component of the existing protocols. The use of effective and efficient protocols and policies can assist in the successful resolution of cases.

When a protocol is established, the partnering agencies can incorporate it into their agency guidelines to refer to in the event of an AMBER Alert or an EMA. A paper and/or electronic field form can help an investigator make note of important information while on the scene. It is important to remember that AMBER Alerts and EMAs are tools in a missing child investigation strategy. Development of a comprehensive investigative strategy requires careful consideration and planning.

The National Center for Missing & Exploited Children's (NCMEC's) publication *Missing and Abducted Children: A Law Enforcement Guide to Case Investigations and Program Management* describes different types of missing and abduction cases and provides checklists that offer step-by-step recommendations for successful case investigation. A free copy is available by calling 1–800–THE–LOST (1–800–843–5678) or visiting www.ncmecpublications.org. In addition, DOJ provides training for all aspects of cases involving

missing persons and abductions. A list of available DOJ trainings is available at www.amberalert.gov or www.amber-net.org.

Coordinate With the Child Abduction Response Team

The Child Abduction Response Team is a multidisciplinary, multiagency coordinated response to the critical incident of a missing, endangered, and/or abducted child. Upon deployment, and depending on the makeup of the team, CART members can provide expertise in the following areas:

+ Investigative strategies.

+ Technology.

+ Forensics.

+ Search and rescue.

+ Crime intelligence analysis.

+ Other areas involving abducted and endangered children, including reunification and victim advocacy.

Criteria for activating a CART are not limited to the criteria for an AMBER Alert, and similar criteria may be used for an EMA. Task force members should consider activating CARTs when EMAs are issued.

Develop a Major Case-Response Plan

Activating an EMA is a collaborative effort that involves all stakeholders. A 24-hour coordinated response plan should be in place to accommodate a crisis if it occurs. The EMA should include details about who will respond to the event and a review system to help responders know when to scale back the initial response efforts and resources. The investigating agency should do the following:

+ Decide who in the department has the authority to activate or ask for the activation of an

EMA. The names and contact information of the authorized personnel should be readily available and clearly posted within the agency.

◆ Obtain the following information for the form that will be distributed to broadcasters and the public:

- Name, age, and physical description of the endangered missing person.

- Description of the person's clothing.

- Location and time that the person was last seen.

- Description of any vehicle that may be involved in the abduction or disappearance.

- Description of possible suspects.

- Last known direction of travel and possible destination.

- The investigating law enforcement agency and telephone number to call to report information about the case.

- The media representative's name and contact information; it is critical to provide this information rather than that for the detective to avoid delays in the investigation.

◆ Once the information about the victim and suspect has been confirmed, it should be provided to the appropriate law enforcement agency and the EMA should be distributed to the media and the public. Activation of the EMA can be authorized only by the law enforcement agency investigating the case or a law enforcement agency that has been designated to issue the advisory for that area.

◆ The investigating agency should obtain the most recent photograph of the endangered missing person as soon as possible. The photograph should be scanned and e-mailed for distribution to the media. Each photograph should receive careful attention to protect the dignity of the individual (e.g., if a child is wearing a bathing suit, a cropped picture of the face only is best).

◆ Consider allocating additional resources. Officers may need to be reassigned from other units and the CART should be notified if it is available. Assistance from other municipal, county, state, and federal agencies may also be needed. A review of mutual aid policies should be considered.

◆ Delegate a media liaison to coordinate information and interviews. The media liaison should be trained to deal with individuals who have no investigative input and he or she should be prepared for the possibility of two media briefings a day in high-profile cases.

Coordinate Activation of the Plan

The task force should consider adopting or modifying elements of the AMBER Alert plan to activate an EMA. The following methods may be modified for an EMA:

◆ **E-mail notification.** A Web portal or listserv will help ensure that the advisory e-mails go out in a timely manner.

◆ **Blast fax.** Many plans use the Lost Child Alert Technology Resource (LOCATER) or other systems to send thousands of fliers with information and photographs. For more information on LOCATER, visit www.locaterposters.org.

◆ **Automatic phone notification.** This method can be used to contact thousands of residents in the area in which the person went missing. A number of task forces use a company called "A Child is Missing" to accomplish this task. For more information, visit www.achildismissing.org.

◆ **National Weather Service (NWS).** The NWS can send the EMA over its radio system. The NWS has sent AMBER Alerts over the radio at the request of state and local officials. This method should only be considered as a back-up to other means of notification.

The task force should also determine whether it would be beneficial to distribute information through other means that are used for AMBER Alerts. For example, the task force should consider the benefits and disadvantages of sending the EMA through the following means:

✦ **Emergency Alert System (EAS).** The EAS has been used to send EMA messages using the Administrative Message code (the Child Abduction Emergency code can only be used for AMBER Alerts). Broadcasters do not always pay attention to the Administrative Message, so this method should only be considered as a backup means of notification.

✦ **Variable message signs.** Electronic highway signs are also known as variable message signs and are usually used to notify motorists about traffic emergencies. The signs have been used for AMBER Alerts and may be considered for EMAs.

✦ **Highway Advisory Radio (HAR).** These low-power AM radio signals provide traffic information to motorists. The HAR has been used for AMBER Alerts and may be considered for EMAs.

✦ **Lottery tickets.** Many states post information about missing and abducted persons on lottery terminals and print information for lottery customers. NOTE: When tickets are printed there are no means of cancellation.

✦ **Service providers.** Trucking associations, taxicabs, school bus programs, delivery and repair services, and other businesses may help in the search.

✦ **Business signs.** Many businesses include AMBER Alerts on commercial signs and may be willing to include EMAs.

✦ **Movie theaters.** Some theaters will include AMBER Alerts and EMAs on the screen before a film begins.

Establish an EMA Protocol for News Agencies

Each jurisdiction should decide how frequently the EMA will be used. Some will treat the EMA as a "super press release" and will use it often to notify the public when a person is missing. Others will save it for more serious cases. Broadcasters are urged to notify the public about every EMA. However, broadcasters will determine on a case-by-case basis whether to break into programming and how much airtime to devote to the situation.

When a news agency is involved in an EMA plan, it needs to develop a protocol for responding to the advisory. Time is critical because the more quickly the information is distributed to the community, the more quickly the case can be resolved. Once stations agree to be a part of the plan, they will broadcast the information that the investigating agency sends to them.

Before an EMA is distributed to participating media outlets, each outlet needs to coordinate how it will handle the information and by whom. A chain of command should be established to determine how the system will work so that an advisory can be broadcast as quickly as possible.

Television and radio stations should decide if designated personnel will break into programming immediately or wait for the first natural break in programming or until the next scheduled news broadcast. (Using wording such as "broadcasting during the first natural break" helps promote the EMA in a manner that does not interfere with normal programming.) When the television and/or radio stations receive information, personnel will either read the copy as written or rewrite it in broadcast style, including all information that law enforcement provides. Since news outlets are not staffed 24 hours a day, a protocol should be developed to ensure the consistency of the plan.

Decide on a Review Board

Members of the EMA task force can also serve as a review board for each EMA. An EMA may be used more often than an AMBER Alert because the criteria are broader and fit many more situations. Task force members should monitor the use of each EMA to track successes and failures. This will also help determine when a plan may need modifications as well as determine training needs and performance measures.

Develop and Implement Training for Law Enforcement and the Media

For an EMA to be effective, it is essential to provide training for law enforcement and the media, including broadcasters, before an announcement to the public takes place. Some states incorporate the EMA in their AMBER Alert training sessions and training materials. Scenario-based practical exercises are a good way to let law enforcement and the media know that alternatives are available when a case does not meet the AMBER Alert criteria.

Test the EMA Plan

A test of the EMA should be conducted with law enforcement and broadcasters to confirm that the advisory works. When testing the advisory, the standardized form should be highlighted to reflect that this is a test and not an actual case of an endangered missing person.

The test should be used only with the equipment and personnel needed during an EMA. The EMA test should not be broadcast because this might create confusion with an AMBER Alert, which requires immediate broadcast notifications.

Coordinate Press Announcements

An official press announcement can be made after the plan has been tested. A news conference can also be held to explain to the public how the EMA works. The press conference should include representatives from the task force and, if possible, a parent or victim to speak out about the need for an EMA. All press and media events should be used to educate the public on EMAs and AMBER

Alerts. The public will want to know about the differences between them. Sample press releases are shown in appendix 4.

Public service announcements can also be used to help educate the public.

Develop Contact Lists

Communities should already have a complete list of law enforcement agencies and media outlets that participate in the AMBER Alert plan (NCMEC should be included in the list if the missing person is younger than age 21). The list can be used or modified for the EMA. Telephone numbers, fax numbers, and e-mail addresses should be compiled and updated regularly to make sure the advisory can be disseminated quickly. NCMEC can be reached through the 24-hour hotline at 1–800–THE–LOST (1–800–843–5678), by e-mail at hotline@ncmec.org, or by fax at 703–274–2096.

Activating an EMA

Following are important points when activating an EMA:

+ Establish phone banks.

+ Notify law enforcement personnel.

+ Notify NCMEC.

+ Prepare for community reaction and response.

+ Prepare for media reaction.

+ Determine media responsibilities.

+ Provide confidential phone and fax lines and e-mail addresses.

+ Review activations.

Establish Phone Banks

Before activating an EMA, it is critical that a hotline telephone bank be set up and staffed. Agencies should be positioned to receive and process incoming leads, and hotline volunteers and personnel should be in place to take calls.

The law enforcement agency is responsible for assigning a telephone number for the EMA; the number can be made public when an advisory goes out. To avoid dropped calls, the number should be able to roll over into several separate lines to handle a large number of calls. In addition, every phone call should be tape recorded. No matter who answers the calls, a supervisor and an investigator should be present at the phone bank. It is critical for those who staff the phone bank to capture, maintain, and disseminate all leads to the proper personnel to ensure that no lead or call is missed.

Notify Law Enforcement Personnel

A supervisor within the law enforcement agency should be responsible for notifying agency personnel about the EMA and should be prepared to provide the details of the case.

Notify NCMEC

NCMEC should be notified if the victim is younger than age 21. This can be done through the 24-hour hotline at 1–800–THE–LOST (1–800–843–5678), by e-mail at hotline@ncmec.org, or by fax at 703–274–2096.

Prepare for Community Reaction and Response

The reaction from the community may be intense and overwhelming because most people want to help. It is important to be able to explain how an EMA is different from an AMBER Alert and that it can be just as effective in bringing a missing person home safely.

If viewers or listeners call the media and request an EMA, local news staff should refer callers to their local law enforcement agency to report the missing endangered person. News staff can explain to callers that *only* law enforcement decides whether to activate an EMA.

Prepare for Media Reaction

Once the EMA is activated, media coverage can be overwhelming in some cases, especially for small law enforcement departments. A public information officer (PIO) should be appointed to work with the press. This will allow the chief executive officer who is overseeing the case to concentrate on the investigation.

The PIO must be informed about the most current information so that he or she can provide the media with daily updates and media releases. PIOs should use the media as much as possible to receive maximum exposure for the case.

Determine Media Responsibilities

In any news organization, a report of an endangered missing person is often considered a breaking story. As with the AMBER Alert, each news outlet should have a coordinated plan that brings together the engineering, production, talent, and news-gathering departments. Although the media do not participate in the decisionmaking process that triggers an EMA, broadcasters, cable systems, and media outlets are critical to the program's success. All members of the news staff should be aware of how the EMA works and understand the format by which the advisory will be sent out.

Provide Confidential Phone and Fax Lines and E-Mail Addresses

Media outlets should have a confidential phone and fax line as well as an e-mail address from law enforcement to receive an EMA. This will eliminate the potential problem of false or misleading information being distributed. Authorized law enforcement personnel will maintain the confidential information. There should be more than one communication method in case one system is down (e.g., if the computer system is down, faxing the information should be an option).

Review Activations

After an EMA is activated, agencies should be prepared to provide a report to the EMA task force. The report should include reasons why the advisory was issued, details about what worked or did not work during the activation, and under what conditions the endangered missing person was found.

The task force should then use the report to help determine any modifications needed to make the EMA more effective. Because investigations may be ongoing, law enforcement agencies may choose to divulge some of the information in person rather than putting it into a report that could be made public.

Building and Sustaining the EMA Plan

To build and sustain the EMA plan, the following must take place:

+ Build community awareness.

+ Obtain sponsorships.

+ Involve other stakeholders.

+ Create awareness.

Build Community Awareness

Law enforcement agencies, the media, and broadcast agencies can educate the public on what to do when a person is missing and is believed to be in danger. For example, the public should know to call 911 immediately and also contact their local law enforcement agency. The law enforcement agency that answers the call should obtain detailed information from the caller regarding the circumstances of the missing person and any details about a potential suspect. The public should be taught what to do when they receive notices

about these alerts and they should understand the difference between EMAs and AMBER Alerts.

Key community leaders on the task force, as well as the missing children clearinghouse in each state, can impart useful information to the public and raise community awareness about EMAs. To find the missing children clearinghouse in each state, visit www.missingkids.com/lawenforcement and click on "Missing-Child Clearinghouse Program." The clearinghouses can conduct presentations and distribute brochures to area civic organizations, schools, safety fairs, and other appropriate venues.

Obtain Sponsorships

Private-sector companies often want to attach themselves to the AMBER Alert and the EMA. Corporate partners can help underwrite the cost of brochures and videotapes for community awareness. To maintain the credibility of the plan, names of sponsors and supporters should not be included in EMA broadcasts.

Involve Other Stakeholders

Communities can encourage local businesses to become involved in the EMA. Examples include municipal and school bus programs, taxi and delivery companies, couriers, repair services, and other companies and agencies that employ drivers who can help in a search. Other businesses such as movie theaters can help distribute information about an EMA.

Create Awareness

Creating awareness for the EMA can be done in a manner similar to the AMBER Alert. To enhance visibility of the EMA, task forces should work with their partners to develop materials such as the following:

+ Brochures.

+ Posters (showing criteria, activation procedures, and other information) that can be displayed in breakrooms at law enforcement agencies and broadcaster outlets.

+ Talking points for officers, broadcasters, and community liaisons who speak about the EMA.

+ Informational booths at safety and community fairs.

+ Promotional items.

+ News segments about past activations, success stories, and general information about how the plan works.

+ Pocket-size activation cards for law enforcement.

+ Editorials about the importance of the EMA.

+ Radio and television public service announcements.

+ Information from the EMA task force's Web site with links to partnering agencies.

Conclusion

The Endangered Missing Advisory is the next step in law enforcement efforts to help recover missing persons safely. The AMBER Alert plan will continue to be used to recover abducted children, and the EMA will be used for other individuals who are missing and endangered.

Communities will benefit from having a single, clear plan that can be used in all cases that do not fit the AMBER Alert criteria. Establishing a plan will also ensure that there is no confusion over numerous alerts and advisories that differ

because of the age of the person or the circumstances of the case. The mission is simple: to use all available tools within reach to save lives.

References

Alzheimer's Association Statement on Silver Alert. July 15, 2008. Available from www.alz.org/news_and_events_14004.asp.

Donnellan, J. 2001. *AMBER Alert Law Enforcement and Broadcaster Guide.* Washington, DC: U.S. Department of Justice, Office of Justice Programs, Office of Juvenile Justice and Delinquency Prevention.

McKenna, R. 2006. *Case Management for Missing Children Homicide Investigation.* Washington, DC: U.S. Department of Justice, Office of Justice Programs, Office of Juvenile Justice and Delinquency Prevention.

Murphy, P. 2009. Survey on Endangered Missing Persons. Unpublished. Appleton, WI: Fox Valley Technical College.

National Center for Missing & Exploited Children. 2007. *2007 AMBER Alert Report.* Washington, DC: U.S. Department of Justice, Office of Justice Programs, Office of Juvenile Justice and Delinquency Prevention.

Office of Juvenile Justice and Delinquency Prevention. 2002. *Highlights From the NISMART Bulletins.* Washington, DC: U.S. Department of Justice, Office of Justice Programs, Office of Juvenile Justice and Delinquency Prevention.

Washington State Office of the Attorney General. 1997. *State Attorney General Releases Homicide Study.* Press Release (May 13, 1997).

Appendix I. Resources

State Clearinghouses

All states have clearinghouses that offer community assistance in missing person cases. When developing an Endangered Missing Advisory (EMA) plan, the best procedure is to work closely with the state clearinghouse and determine what resources are available. Many clearinghouses provide law enforcement with opportunities for networking and training and methods for information dissemination, data collection, and technical assistance.

The National Center for Missing & Exploited Children (NCMEC) instructs clearinghouse personnel to submit missing children cases directly to the NCMEC Web site at www.missingkids.com. In addition, www.missingkids.com/lawenforcement (click on "Missing-Child Clearinghouse Program" under Featured Services) includes contact information for each state. NCMEC's 24-hour call center at 1–800–THE–LOST (1–800–843–5678) can also provide contact information for each state clearinghouse.

State Departments of Transportation

State departments of transportation are likely to be key partners in the AMBER Alert Program and can be a valuable partner for the EMA. The departments can assist with variable message signs, Highway Advisory Radio, or 511 traffic information lines to notify the public about an EMA. Each state determines whether the signs can be used for an AMBER Alert, EMA, or any other nontraffic-related message.

The U.S. Department of Transportation has also developed guidelines for posting AMBER Alerts, national security notices, and other nontraffic-related messages on highway signs (www.amberalert.gov/dotinfo.htm). According to the guidelines, the messages must provide the following:

+ Relevant information about the incident.

+ Information to help identify the suspect's vehicle.

+ Information to help locate the victim.

+ Details about how to get more information.

The complete report can be found at www.ops.fhwa.dot.gov.

U.S. Department of Justice

The U.S. Department of Justice (DOJ), Office of Justice Programs (OJP), Office of Juvenile Justice and Delinquency Prevention (OJJDP) develops materials and provides training for the AMBER Alert Program. The program encourages:

+ Using national standards and best practices.

+ Enhancing the use of technology.

+ Coordinating the efforts of law enforcement, transportation, and the media.

+ Increasing public participation through targeted education and increased communication.

+ Sharing resources.

OJP develops materials and provides training to encourage states to incorporate the EMA into their missing person recovery plans. For more information, visit www.usdoj.gov/ojp (click on "Juvenile Justice" under OJP Topics).

National Center for Missing & Exploited Children

NCMEC is a private, nonprofit organization working in cooperation with DOJ to serve as a clearinghouse for information on child victimization issues. Visit www.missingkids.com or call 1–800–THE–LOST (1–800–843–5678) for the following resources:

9-1-1 communication centers. NCMEC provides technical assistance, training, and educational materials to help 9-1-1 communication centers respond effectively to reports of missing and/or sexually exploited children. For more information, visit www.missingkids.com/en_US/documents/911CallCenterHistory.pdf.

AMBER Alert. Together with DOJ, NCMEC offers technical assistance and training to all AMBER Alert plans. The center also disseminates AMBER Alert messages to distributors of secondary communications through the AMBER Alert Secondary Distribution Program. This program enhances AMBER Alert activations for law enforcement and the general public and has been widely expanded to include various Internet providers, outdoor digital signage systems, coordinated highway networks, and public and private employers. For more information, visit www.amberalert.gov or www.missingkids.com/amber.

Case analysis. Using NCMEC databases, external sources, and geographic databases, analysts track leads, identify patterns among cases, and help coordinate investigations by linking cases together.

Family advocacy services. NCMEC provides technical assistance, referrals, and crisis intervention services for families, law enforcement, and family advocacy agencies.

Family reunification assistance. NCMEC can help arrange transportation free of charge to reunite children with families who have exhausted personal resources during the search process. This service is made possible through NCMEC's private-sector transportation partners—American Airlines, Amtrak, Continental Airlines, and Greyhound.

Forensic assistance. NCMEC provides age-progressed photographs of missing children; reconstructed facial images of unidentified, deceased children; and assistance to families, law enforcement, and medical examiners to resolve long-term missing children cases.

Hotline (1–800–THE–LOST or 1–800–843–5678). NCMEC operates the hotline 24 hours a day, 7 days a week to record leads and other information from the public, help professionals and families who are searching for missing children, and assist in sexual exploitation cases.

Infant abduction prevention program. NCMEC provides infant abduction prevention training to nursing associations, hospital security associations, and law enforcement agencies. NCMEC also provides investigative assistance to law enforcement on infant abduction cases.

International family abduction services. NCMEC assists families, law enforcement, attorneys, and others in finding and recovering children who are the victims of international abduction.

LOCATER. NCMEC's Lost Child Alert Technology Resource enables law enforcement to rapidly create and disseminate posters of missing children locally, statewide, and nationwide.

Missing-Child Clearinghouse Program. All 50 states, the District of Columbia, Puerto Rico, the U.S. Virgin Islands, Canada, Greece, and the Netherlands provide resources for missing children, their families, and the professionals who serve them. NCMEC provides training and technical support to assist with missing children investigations.

Photo and poster distribution. NCMEC provides national media exposure of missing children cases through partnerships with television networks, nationwide publications, and corporate partners.

Project ALERT. NCMEC coordinates America's Law Enforcement Retiree Team, which is composed of skilled, retired law enforcement officers who provide free, onsite assistance to active law enforcement officers.

Team Adam. Team Adam sends experienced investigative specialists to the sites of serious child abductions and child sexual exploitation cases to advise and assist local investigators. Team Adam also provides rapid, onsite assistance to law enforcement agencies and families in cases of missing, abducted, and exploited children. Its members are retired law enforcement professionals with years of investigative experience at the federal, state, and local levels.

Nonprofit Organizations

Collaborating with other local nonprofit organizations can assist in the goal of finding missing persons. Nonprofit organizations are vital in promoting information and sharing it with other grassroots organizations. These groups can also help law enforcement mobilize volunteers to help in searches or distribute posters.

The Association of Missing and Exploited Children's Organizations (AMECO) maintains a resource and referral list of nonprofit organizations for OJJDP. The list includes organizations throughout the United States and Canada that provide direct services to families of missing and exploited children. AMECO also oversees these organizations to help ensure they carry out their mission in an ethical and legitimate manner. For more information about becoming a member of AMECO, visit www.amecoinc.org.

Appendix 2. Endangered Missing Advisory Examples

The following examples are cases in which an Endangered Missing Advisory (EMA) was issued.

Ben Ownby and Shawn Hornbeck

On January 8, 2007, 13-year-old Ben Ownby got off a schoolbus at 3:45 p.m. with a friend, but he never made it home. Ben's father called for help and the sheriff considered issuing an AMBER Alert at 7:15 p.m. However, law enforcement officers could not find anyone who saw where Ben went and they did not have any proof he had been abducted. Authorities did not have enough evidence to issue an AMBER Alert, but Missouri had just created an EMA plan and decided to put the new advisory to the test.

The state's first EMA went out at 8:24 p.m. Law enforcement was notified through teletype message channels, and the media received the advisory through the public information officer's media e-mail list. The media coverage was extensive, and hundreds of leads started coming in for the missing boy. A young student came forward and told police he saw the boy being pushed into a white pickup truck. Twelve hours after the advisory went out, authorities had enough information to issue an AMBER Alert. Three days later, deputies spotted a white pickup truck that matched the witness's description. The deputies searched the truck owner's apartment and found Ben Ownby and Shawn Hornbeck, a 15-year-old boy who had been missing since 2002.

Missouri law enforcement authorities were overjoyed that the EMA helped find a boy who had been missing for several days as well as another boy who had been missing for more than 4 years.

Destiny Norton

On July 16, 2006, 5-year-old Destiny Norton walked out of her parents' apartment at about 8:15 p.m. to calm down after arguing with her mother. The little girl, who had silver front teeth and blond hair with green streaks, was wearing her mother's black and grey T-shirt and no shoes. Destiny's parents left the apartment 10 minutes later to look for her. The parents were afraid that something was wrong because Destiny usually would not cross the street and avoided strangers. They called the police and organized a neighborhood search with the help of their church leader, who was also a Salt Lake City, UT, police officer. Police later canvassed the neighborhood for Destiny.

At about 10 p.m., Destiny's father confronted a man who was acting suspiciously. The man had been seen driving around at a slow speed; he had toys in the back of his car and was seen putting something into a dumpster. Police stopped the suspect that night and impounded his car for a registration violation, but did not make any connection between him and Destiny. Authorities found out later the man had been charged and acquitted of two counts of sexually abusing children in 2003.

At 11:30 p.m., police used an automatic phone-dialing service to send 1,000 calls to notify neighbors about the missing child. The FBI was contacted and a joint investigation into a missing/kidnapped child began at 3:30 a.m.

Police decided that the information about the accused sexual offender combined with the age and circumstances of Destiny's disappearance were enough to issue an AMBER Alert. The alert went out at 6:45 a.m. through radio, television, electronic highway signs, 511, Web sites, cell phone, and e-mail to people who had registered to receive the alerts.

The suspect's family saw the AMBER Alert and the suspect turned himself into police at 8:30 a.m. The suspect failed the polygraph twice, but his family offered a strong alibi regarding his whereabouts. Police were not convinced the suspect was the person who took Destiny.

The Salt Lake City police cancelled the alert at noon, but detectives were still concerned that the young girl was in danger and issued an EMA. Police wanted the public's help to find Destiny and wanted everyone to know they still suspected foul play. Hundreds of people volunteered to help in the search and reporters gave a great deal of attention to Destiny's disappearance. The media continued to cover the case as a major news story. Rewards were offered and the public response continued to be the same as if an AMBER Alert was still in effect.

On the evening of July 23, a convenience store clerk in Farmington (about 20 miles north of Salt Lake City) said he saw a girl matching Destiny's description with a man in a truck.

Police issued a second AMBER Alert for Destiny at 10:52 p.m. on July 23. They set up roadblocks and used a helicopter in the search. A citizen heard the alert and saw a similar truck pull into a trailer park in Salt Lake City. Police then determined that the girl in the truck was not Destiny. The AMBER Alert was cancelled at 2:32 a.m. on July 24. Detectives said the AMBER Alert and the EMA produced a large number of leads for their investigation. The same day, detectives started interviewing and conducting polygraph tests with the Nortons' neighbor, Craig Roger Gregerson. Gregerson failed a polygraph and then admitted that he had something to do with Destiny's death. At the same time, police decided to issue a sketch of the man seen in the truck at the convenience store, based on speculation that the truck in the trailer park was not the truck seen at the convenience store. Police decided not to release the sketch until they received an absolute confession.

Based on information from Gregerson, Destiny's body was found at 8:30 p.m. on July 24 in Gregerson's basement. Her body had been stuffed in a plastic storage box and Gregerson had used cleaning agents to mask the odor. Gregerson told police he could not move the child because of the constant police presence. He pleaded guilty as charged to capital murder and kidnapping. On December 5, 2006, Gregerson was sentenced to life in prison without parole for Destiny's murder and another 15 years to life for her kidnapping.

Malcolm Jamal Baker and Eric Lerma

On June 10, 2007, the Clinton, UT, police department issued an EMA for an 8-year-old boy and a 9-year-old boy. Malcolm Jamal Baker and Eric Lerma were last seen at 10:30 a.m. playing near their home. The parents looked for the boys at 11 a.m. and reported the matter to police at 5 p.m.

A neighbor reported seeing the boys about 2 miles from their home at about 1 p.m. The police did not suspect foul play but they believed the boys were in danger and started checking covered boats and the trunks of cars as a precaution. A large irrigation canal was also searched. An automated phone message was sent to area residents to alert them that the boys were missing. Police then issued an EMA because they did not believe the case met the AMBER Alert criteria.

Police officers tracked the boys' movements to a hardware store and employees at a nearby store reported that the boys had been there most of the day. The boys had also been seen near a movie theater and a restaurant. At 9 p.m., as daylight was beginning to fade, about 15 search and rescuers from the sheriff's office scoured neighborhoods, trails, and streets in the area. An hour later, there were 75–100 searchers. Twelve hours after the boys went missing, they were found safe near an outdoor shed at the hardware store parking lot. The boys had traveled more than 7 miles from their home on their scooters. At 11 p.m., Clinton police received word of the boys' whereabouts and sent home more than 170 volunteers who were participating in the search.

Vanessa Luren Ochoa

On September 25, 2008, the Midvale, UT, police department issued an EMA for 7-week-old Vanessa Luren Ochoa after she was abducted from the hospital. The child had been placed in state custody after she was born with a cocaine dependency. The baby's mother, Sheila Crump, had lost parental rights of four other children but was allowed visitation with Vanessa. The mother was staying at a treatment center and was allowed to take Vanessa to the hospital for treatment for dehydration. However, the hospital staff were unaware that Crump did not have the right to leave the hospital with her baby.

The police had evidence that the child had been abducted but did not believe the child was in imminent danger, so they issued an EMA instead of an AMBER Alert. Based on phone calls and tips, the police were able to trace Crump to her mother's house in Johnson City, TN. Crump was charged with kidnapping, and her baby was returned to Utah and placed in foster care.

Deborah Jones

On April 21, 2008, Salt Lake City police issued an EMA for 50-year-old Deborah Jones. She had broken up with her boyfriend 2 weeks earlier and had contacted police because he was making violent threats. Ms. Jones' family became concerned after she failed to turn up for work and her cell phone had been turned off. Family members said the missing woman was very detail oriented and would never leave without letting someone know about it. The media covered the story extensively. A neighbor of the suspect called police and said that the suspect may have taken a mentally handicapped woman as well. The next day, police in Branson, MO, found Ms. Jones' car and her body inside it.

The ex-boyfriend and the handicapped woman were found alive in a hotel room. Detectives say the EMA did not go out in time to save Ms. Jones but that it likely saved the other woman from harm.

Christopher Stone

On October 11, 2007, Tennessee authorities issued an EMA for 1-year-old Christopher Stone. The boy had been taken by his noncustodial father and police believed the child was in danger. The father was wanted after he took the child with him during a high-speed chase and escaped after crashing his car into a patrol car. The media provided extensive coverage on the case and the child was found unharmed 3 days later.

The following are cases in which an EMA could have been considered.

Mary Zelter

On February 26, 2008, 86-year-old Mary Zelter signed herself out of her assisted living center and went shopping. Ms. Zelter suffered from bouts of dementia, and the family became concerned when she did not return home. Police issued a BOLO (Be On the Look Out) to other law enforcement agencies and the media. Worried family members flew in from around the country, distributed posters, and held rallies to solicit the public's help.

The media attention helped generate leads, and police learned that the missing woman had used her credit card an hour after she left the center but did not use it again. Her body was found in a waterway a week later; her automobile was also retrieved. Ms. Zelter's death inspired federal legislation to support states that want to set up Silver Alerts to find missing senior citizens.

Julie Kay Webster

On August 1, 2002, law enforcement officials began a search after a 58-year-old woman went missing in Wyoming. Julie Kay Webster had early-onset Alzheimer's disease and was last seen 3 days earlier on a surveillance tape buying gasoline at a gas station. Ms. Webster was supposed to pick up her daughter at Minneapolis-St. Paul International Airport, but she never showed up. Ms. Webster was found dead in a ravine on August 2, less than a mile from her car. She had apparently walked away after her car became stuck in sage brush.

Norman and Yvonne Olson

Norman and Yvonne Olson, residents of Hettinger, ND, were last seen on August 14, 2004. Neighbors had noticed that the lights had been left on in their house and the garden and flower beds were starting to dry up. The couple's children became concerned because the front door was locked and the couple never locked the door. Norman Olson was being treated for depression, had recently been diagnosed with Alzheimer's disease, and was suffering from short-term memory loss. The Olsons' children broke into the garage and discovered their parents' car was missing.

They also found a package of meat on the kitchen counter that had become rancid and a coffee maker that had burnt out after being left on. A .22 caliber revolver was believed to be missing but there was no sign of a struggle. Police and family organized searches and volunteers used aircraft and horses to scour the area. In November, the bodies of the couple were found in an abandoned house. Authorities determined that Norman Olson killed his wife and then committed suicide.

DeMond Tunstall, Ivan Tunstall-Collins, and Jinella Tunstall

On September 23, 2006, East St. Louis, IL, police found Jimella Tunstall dead. Her abdomen had been torn apart and the pregnant woman's fetus was missing. Authorities contacted the media when they learned that the victim's children (7-year-old DeMond Tunstall, 2-year-old Ivan Tunstall-Collins, and 1-year-old Jinella Tunstall) were also missing.

Investigators carried out a search and discovered the children were last seen with a family friend. Police found the family friend, who admitted to killing the mother to get her baby. She also told officers where to find the other children. Police went back to the victim's apartment and found the dead children, whose bodies were decomposing inside the washer and dryer.

The following are additional cases in which various types of alerts were issued:

On November 2, 2000, police issued a crime alert after a father abducted his 5-month-old child during a domestic disturbance. The alert was sent to other law enforcement agencies, motels, clinics, and airports. A hotel employee recognized the suspect and the child when the father tried to check into a room. The employee contacted the police and the child was returned to the mother unharmed.

On November 4, 2005, a 24-year-old woman was grabbed by her ponytail and forced into the car of her former boyfriend. The ex-boyfriend had a history of violence and the family feared the victim was in danger. Police issued an EMA and, with help from the public, the suspect's car and the victim were located in less than 2 hours.

On May 5, 2006, police issued an EMA at 5:10 a.m. for a 7-year-old boy with mental problems and medical needs that required medication. The boy was last seen at 10 p.m. the previous night. Broadcasters aired the advisory; a neighbor realized that the boy, who said he had permission to stay at their house, was the same boy mentioned in the advisory. The mother and child were reunited.

On May 22, 2006, a 14-year-old girl sent a text message to her family and friends claiming she had been kidnapped and that her abductors were demanding ransom. Police were skeptical because the ransom amount was very low and the girl had a history of running away with her boyfriend. Officers decided to be on the safe side and issued an EMA to notify the public and other law enforcement agencies. The girl was found a short time later and she admitted the kidnapping was a hoax.

On January 19, 2007, police issued an EMA for a missing 86-year-old man who was known to become easily confused when he had not taken his medication for diabetes. The man was last seen driving an older model truck with the rear window missing. The public was able to help authorities locate the missing man hundreds of miles away from his home.

On October 9, 2007, a sheriff issued an EMA for two teens who ran away from a youth detention center. One teen was a diabetic and had not taken his medication for 36 hours. The other teen had a history of assaulting people with a deadly weapon. Both of them had a history of stealing vehicles and being involved in high-speed pursuits. The boys had also told some people that they planned to steal a vehicle. Law enforcement authorities found the juveniles in another town less than 6 hours after the advisory went out.

On October 10, 2007, a 3-year-old girl went missing near a marina at a large lake. Witnesses saw the girl near the covered boat slips around noon. Some witnesses said they had seen the girl, and

the sheriff issued an EMA at 5:57 p.m. Hundreds of people joined in the search for the girl; her body was found in the lake the following afternoon.

On November 7, 2007, police issued a crime alert for a missing 16-year-old girl. The alert was posted at many gas stations and other locations and generated many leads. The girl was found unharmed the next day.

On November 13, 2007, police issued an EMA for a missing 42-year-old woman. The woman was depressed and had threatened to commit suicide. She had numerous medical conditions and had left with numerous antidepressants. The woman was found dead in a ravine 2 days later.

On November 30, 2007, police issued an EMA for a 26-year-old woman. Police feared she was in danger because she had the mental capacity of a 7-year-old. The public helped locate the woman less than an hour after the advisory went out.

Appendix 3. Sample Plans

Utah

What a Law Enforcement Officer Should Do To Initiate an EMA

Purpose. The Endangered Missing Advisory (EMA) is a voluntary partnership between law enforcement and local broadcasters to rapidly disseminate information about a missing and endangered person to law enforcement agencies, broadcasters, and the public.

Criteria. Only Utah law enforcement agencies can initiate an EMA, using the following criteria:

✦ Do the circumstances fail to meet the criteria for an AMBER Alert? (If they meet the criteria, immediately follow the protocol to issue an AMBER Alert.)

✦ Is the person missing under unexplained, involuntary, or suspicious circumstances?

✦ Is the person believed to be in danger because of age, health, mental or physical disability, or environment or weather conditions; because they are in the company of a potentially dangerous person; or some other factor that may put the person in peril?

✦ Is there information that could assist the public in the safe recovery of the missing person?

Procedure for Agencies To Initiate an EMA

If all criteria are met, prepare the "Endangered Missing Advisory" by using the Attempt To Locate (ATL) code on the Utah Criminal Justice Information System (UCJIS). Write "Endangered Missing Advisory" in the title of the entry. A Field EMA Information Form is available to help you gather information. Contact the Bureau of Criminal Identification (BCI) at 801–965–4446 to verify it received the advisory via UCJIS.

Enter the information with the National Crime Information Center (NCIC) using the proper message key: Missing (MNP), Endangered (EME), Involuntary (EMI). Make sure dispatchers are prepared to handle phone calls.

Consider allocating additional resources from other law enforcement agencies. Obtain a photograph of the missing person and/or suspect as soon as possible and e-mail it to endangered@utah.gov.

A Public Information Officer (PIO) should be appointed to handle the press. Once the advisory has been activated, media coverage may be overwhelming, especially for a small department. The PIO should be constantly updated so he or she can use the media as much as possible and receive the maximum exposure for the case.

The EMA does not preclude the use of any in-house procedures, policies, or practices established by discrete law enforcement agencies.

The following will happen after the advisory is activated:

✦ All Utah law enforcement agencies are notified through UCJIS.

✦ Broadcasters and the media are notified by e-mail.

✦ Thousands of flyers with photos and details are distributed to businesses throughout Utah and surrounding states.

✦ Ports of entry inform all of their officers.

✦ The National Center for Missing & Exploited Children (NCMEC) is contacted if the person is younger than age 18.

Additional Resources

BCI can contact other states if the advisory needs to be sent outside of Utah. BCI is also available to provide training or training materials. Call 801–965–4446.

The Utah Public Information Officer Association can provide a PIO to help your agency. Call 801–541–8145 or 801–554–5422.

A Child Is Missing (ACIM) will use an automated telephone system to contact residents and businesses in the area where the person was last seen. The service is free and can be used for a missing child or an elderly or disabled person. Call 888–875–ACIM (888–875–2246).

Team Adam provides experienced child abduction investigators, technical assistance, and equipment free to agencies during investigations involving missing, abducted, or exploited children. Call 1–800–THE–LOST (1–800–843–5678).

Project ALERT provides retired federal, state, and local law enforcement officers, who volunteer their time and expertise as unpaid consultants during investigations of missing, abducted, or exploited children. NCMEC pays for all travel arrangements and costs. Call 1–800–THE–LOST (1–800–843–5678).

Laura Recovery Center will help organize community ground searches. The nonprofit organization offers its services at no cost. Call 866–898–5723.

Canceling the EMA

The initiating agency must cancel the EMA using the UCJIS (ATL) message. The agency must also call BCI at 801–965–4446 to verify that the EMA cancellation notice has been received via UCJIS.

North Carolina Silver Alert Program

What Is a Silver Alert?

Silver Alert is a system to quickly notify the public about missing endangered adults who suffer from dementia or other cognitive impairments. Since adults with these mental ailments often become confused and disoriented, it is imperative that they are found quickly and returned to their caregivers.

Developed in 2007, the program is a cooperative effort among local and state law enforcement and the North Carolina Center for Missing Persons (NCCMP), with voluntary participation by radio and television broadcasters and the North Carolina Department of Transportation. The Silver Alert program is based on the Cognitive Impairment Assistance Law that passed in August 2007; it builds on the success of the state's AMBER Alert system. Although North Carolina's Silver Alert program criteria are unique, two other states have similar programs.

What Are the Criteria?

NCCMP is the only agency that can activate a Silver Alert and will do so only at the request of an investigating law enforcement agency. It is then the responsibility of the center to determine whether there are sufficient data to justify activating the Silver Alert system.

To activate a Silver Alert, the following statutory criteria must be met:

+ The person is 18 years old or older.

+ The person is believed to be suffering from dementia or other cognitive impairments.

+ The person is believed to be missing — regardless of circumstances.

+ A legal custodian of the missing person has submitted a missing person's report to the local law enforcement agency where the person went missing.

How Does It Work?

The investigating local law enforcement agency and NCCMP (800–522–5437, 919–733–3557 (inquiries only), 919–715–1682 (fax), www.nccrimecontrol.org) work together to notify the surrounding community and the media about the missing endangered person.

DO NOT release any health information other than cognitive impairment status.

Law enforcement is responsible for the following:

+ Notify NCCMP.

+ Send completed Silver Alert forms to the center.

+ Enter information into the National Crime Information Center.

+ Initiate a statewide Be On the Look Out.

+ Establish a 24-hour phone number.

+ Activate reverse 911 calls.

+ For walkaways, call A Child Is Missing (888–875–2246, 954–763–4569 (fax), www.achildismissing.org).

+ Notify NCMEC at 1–800–THE–LOST if the missing person is younger than age 21.

NCCMP responsibilities include the following:

+ Activate North Carolina Department of Transportation electronic highway signs (if appropriate).

+ Update the Web site (www.nccrimecontrol.org).

+ Send information to the media.

DO NOT release any health information other than cognitive impairment status.

Ohio Missing Child Alert

Unknown circumstances include the following:

+ Is the victim younger than 18 years old?

+ What are the details about the missing child (i.e., lost, nonwitnessed/nonconfirmed abduction, whereabouts are unknown)?

Missing child alert actions include the following:

+ Send a statewide teletype.

+ Send a media blast e-mail and fax.

+ Send an Ohio trucker's alert.

+ Initiate an A Child Is Missing activation.

+ Activate a law enforcement radio broadcast.

+ Activate a Child Abduction Response Team.

+ Notify secondary notification systems.

+ To initiate a missing child alert, contact the Bureau of Criminal Investigation at 740–845–2224.

Arkansas Level II Activation Criteria and Procedure

If circumstances of the disappearance involving an infant, child, or minor do not meet the criteria to permit activation of a Level I Emergency Alert System (EAS) notification, an alternate form of mass notification may be offered to a local law enforcement agency seeking assistance, as described below.

+ A police chief, sheriff, or authorized commander of a local law enforcement agency should follow the guidelines set forth in the previous policy section, "Level I Alerts Relating to Minimum Reporting Criteria."

- An authorized law enforcement commander must complete the Morgan Nick AMBER Alert System Initial Reporting Form, sign the document, and electronically mail or fax the form to the Arkansas State Police (ASP) Troop A Communications Center.

- Authorization of a Level II alert is delegated to the agency's Criminal Investigation Division commander. In the event the division commander is unavailable, authorization of the alert system will default upward in the ASP chain of command, beginning with the commander of the Criminal Investigation Division. If a Level II notification is authorized, the ASP will disseminate information contained in the initial reporting form, along with a current photograph of the missing infant, child, or minor through the electronic mail server maintained by ASP. Using an ASP e-mail template, a Troop A telecom operator will transcribe the necessary information from the initial reporting form onto the template. The photograph may be included as an attached file or sent separately as the photograph becomes available. The e-mail will be sent to a list of subscribers, to include both print and broadcast newsrooms across the state.

- The e-mail will contain information about the identity of the missing person, a description of the missing person, and information about any possible suspect or person of interest to the law enforcement agency initiating the request. The e-mail message will contain the name of the person who will serve as a primary point of contact within the reporting law enforcement agency and a telephone number where the person can be contacted.

- Notifications by e-mail using the Morgan Nick AMBER Alert System criteria should include a mandatory disclaimer in each transmission, stating: "The following information has been provided to the Arkansas State Police by local law enforcement officers with immediate jurisdiction in this case and does not rise to the reporting level for activation of the Level I Emergency Alert System, Morgan Nick AMBER Alert. The information contained in this advisory and any photographs that follow may be released at the discretion of the Morgan Nick AMBER Alert subscriber. Inquiries should be directed to the local law enforcement agency that has requested the Level II alert."

- Additional information developed from the continued investigation into the disappearance of an infant, child, or minor may warrant reconsideration as to whether to activate the Level I EAS. The Criminal Investigation Division commander may upgrade a Level II alert to a Level I EAS activation.

- Pursuant to applicable Arkansas statutes, release and (or) confirmation of criminal history information, medical history, or personal information relating to the victim and (or) suspect is prohibited.

Minnesota Law Enforcement Checklist

1. Is the abduction one in which the victim is 17 years old or younger?

- If yes, answer question 2.

- If no, answer question 3.

- Do you believe the child to be in imminent danger of serious bodily harm or death?

    - If yes, active the AMBER Plan and the Minnesota Crime Alert Network.

    - If no, do not activate the AMBER Plan; go to question 3.

2. Provide the following information to the Bureau of Criminal Apprehension:

- When/where the child was abducted.

+ A description of the child.

+ A description of the abductor.

+ A description of the vehicle, if one is involved.

+ The last known direction of travel.

+ Is there reason to believe the suspect has a relationship to the victim?

+ Phone number to call for general information and questions.

The police should carefully consider not activating the plan if there is no information to send out.

Could assistance from the public, including other law enforcement agencies, businesses, and the media, help locate an individual who does not qualify for an AMBER Alert?

+ If yes, activate the Minnesota Crime Alert Network.

+ If no, do not activate the Minnesota Crime Alert Network.

3. Could assistance from the public, including other law enforcement agencies, businesses, and the media, help locate an individual who does not qualify for an AMBER Alert?

Appendix 4. Sample Press Releases

For Immediate Release
September 19, 2005

Contact Paul Murphy
Utah Attorney General's Office
801–538–1892
pmurphy@utah.gov

Utah Has a New Tool To Find Missing People

Utah law enforcement officers and broadcasters are once again joining forces to find missing people. Attorney General Mark Shurtleff announced today the launch of the Endangered Missing Advisory (EMA), a new plan to recover missing people who do not fit the criteria for an AMBER Alert.

"The AMBER Alert has been an extremely effective tool for bringing abducted children home. With the addition of the EMA, police officers now have a simple, clear-cut plan to find others who may be in danger," says Shurtleff.

Before issuing an EMA, a law enforcement officer must consider four criteria:

1. Do the circumstances fail to meet the criteria for an AMBER Alert? (If they do meet the criteria for an AMBER Alert, immediately follow the protocol to issue an AMBER Alert.)

2. Is the person missing under unexplained or suspicious circumstances?

3. Is the person in danger because of age, health, mental or physical disability, and environment or weather conditions, or is the person in the company of a potentially dangerous person?

4. Is there information that could assist the public in the safe recovery of the missing person?

The Utah Bureau of Criminal Identification will distribute the advisory to law enforcement, the media, businesses, and ports of entry. Law enforcement can also send the advisory by telephone to residents living in the area where the person was last seen. Information will also go to the National Crime Information Center and the National Center for Missing & Exploited Children if the missing person is under the age of 18.

"Broadcasters want to serve the public and this is another way we can serve and even save lives," says Utah Broadcasters Association President Dale Zabriskie.

An EMA could be used for a number of cases that do not fit the AMBER Alert criteria: a 19-year-old kidnap victim, a 75-year-old Alzheimer's patient, a 14-year-old missing girl with suspicious computer correspondence, or an 11-year-old scout lost in a mountain wilderness area.

"We certainly could have used something like this," says Jody Hawkins, mother of Brennan Hawkins, an 11-year-old who was lost for 4 days in the High Uintas without food or water. "We needed the public's help and we needed it immediately. The EMA will be a real blessing for other parents searching for their children."

Following are some reasons why missing children face serious risks:

✦ A Washington state study found that 68.7 percent of child abduction homicides began as a missing person or runaway case.

✦ The Department of Justice statistics for 2004 indicate that 70 percent of missing children are endangered because of sexual or physical assault, criminal companions, or drug use, or because they are younger than age 13.

✦ A recent series of questions posed to homeless youth in Utah found that 37 percent had been sexually assaulted and 50 percent had attempted suicide.

"The partnership between law enforcement and the media has proven to be a good one with the AMBER Alert. In the same way, the Endangered Missing Advisory will let thousands of people know quickly that someone may be in harm's way," says Woods Cross Police Chief Paul Howard, who represents the Utah Police Chiefs Association for the Utah AMBER Alert Advisory Committee.

A slight change is also being made in the criteria for Utah AMBER Alerts. The Alerts will only be issued for children younger than age 18. The original criteria included an individual with a proven mental or physical disability.

"Utah's criteria are now in line with what the Department of Justice recommends for AMBER Alerts. However, the Utah AMBER Alert Advisory Committee didn't want to make the change until the Endangered Missing Advisory was up and running," says Paul Murphy, spokesperson for the Attorney General's Office and Utah AMBER Alert Coordinator.

The EMA is being initiated on the same day as the fifth test of the Utah AMBER Alert Plan. The tests are held each year on May 25, Missing Children's Day, and September 19, the anniversary of the day kidnap victim Rachael Runyan was found.

"Though it has been 23 years since Rachael's abduction, we still do not forget," says Elaine Runyan-Simmons, mother of Rachael Runyan. "We are still figuring out ways to find our missing children. The fight goes on!"

Attorney General Mike McGrath
State of Montana

For release: June 26, 2008

Contact: Mike Batista or John Strandell, 444–3874

Department of Justice Announces New Missing-Person Advisory Program

HELENA—Montana law enforcement agencies have another tool to find missing children and adults, thanks to a new program in the Division of Criminal Investigation at the Montana Department of Justice.

The new program—the Missing and Endangered Person Advisory, or MEPA (www.doj.mt.gov/enforcement/missingpersons/mepa.asp)—is an alternative to the well-known AMBER Alert Program.

"AMBER Alerts are specifically limited to child abduction cases in which the child's life may be in danger," said Mike Batista, Division of Criminal Investigation (DCI) Administrator.

"AMBER is not meant to track runaways, missing children, children involved in custody disputes, or missing adults, yet those are the types of cases Montana law enforcement agencies deal with."

"MEPA allows agencies to quickly get the word out to the public and to other law enforcement around the state and the region."

The DCI guidelines call for a local agency to first determine whether the case is appropriate for an AMBER Alert. If not, the agency can request an advisory.

DCI will issue the advisory through the National Weather Service, Montana Department of Transportation, and the Montana Lottery.

The media—either in a specific region of the state or statewide—are notified via the Weather Service system or by e-mail or fax.

The requesting agency may also decide to send the advisory to border ports of entry or other public agencies.

If the missing person is younger than age 18, the National Center for Missing & Exploited Children is notified.

The initial advisory will include any available information, such as name, age, physical description, date of birth, and where the person was last seen. It might also include information about whether the person has a health condition or a physical or mental disability.

Generally, the MEPA will expire after 24 hours, although the requesting agency can ask for a longer time period. The advisory can also be updated or cancelled by the requester at any time.

"All of us want to help find missing Montanans, regardless of the circumstances," Batista said. "A program like MEPA will be a useful option for law enforcement."

ADDITIONAL RESOURCES

For more information about the AMBER Alert Program,
including training, technical assistance, and laws,
visit the U.S. Department of Justice Web site at:
www.amberalert.gov

To report an emergency situation or to
provide information about a missing or exploited child,
call 911 to notify your local police or call:
1–800–THE–LOST (1–800–843–5678)

To report information about child pornography,
child molestation, child prostitution, and the
online enticement of children,
log on to the CyberTipline at:
www.cybertipline.com

For more information on missing and
exploited children, visit the National Center for
Missing & Exploited Children (NCMEC) at:
www.missingkids.com